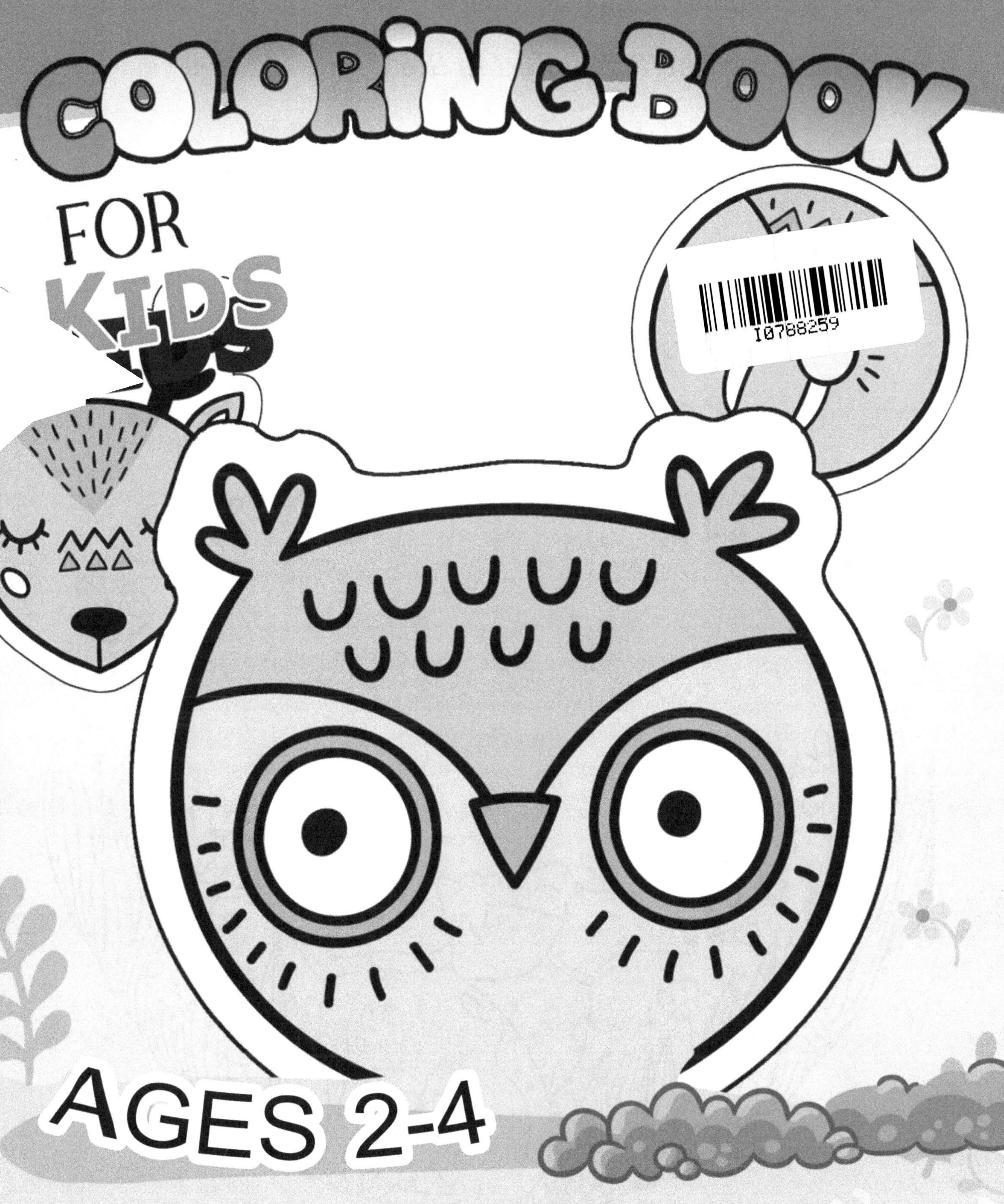

COLORING BOOK
FOR
KIDS
AGES 2-4

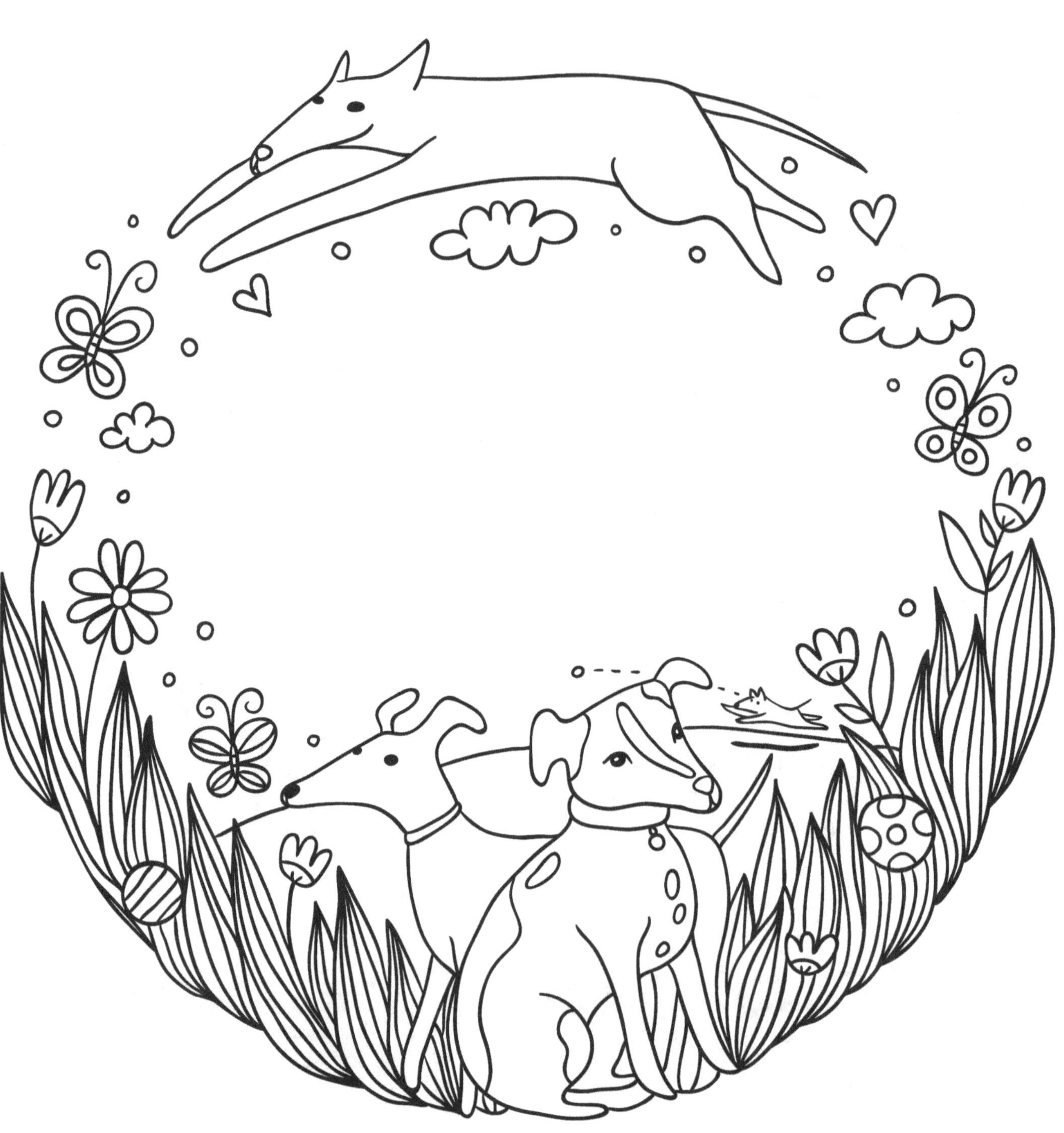

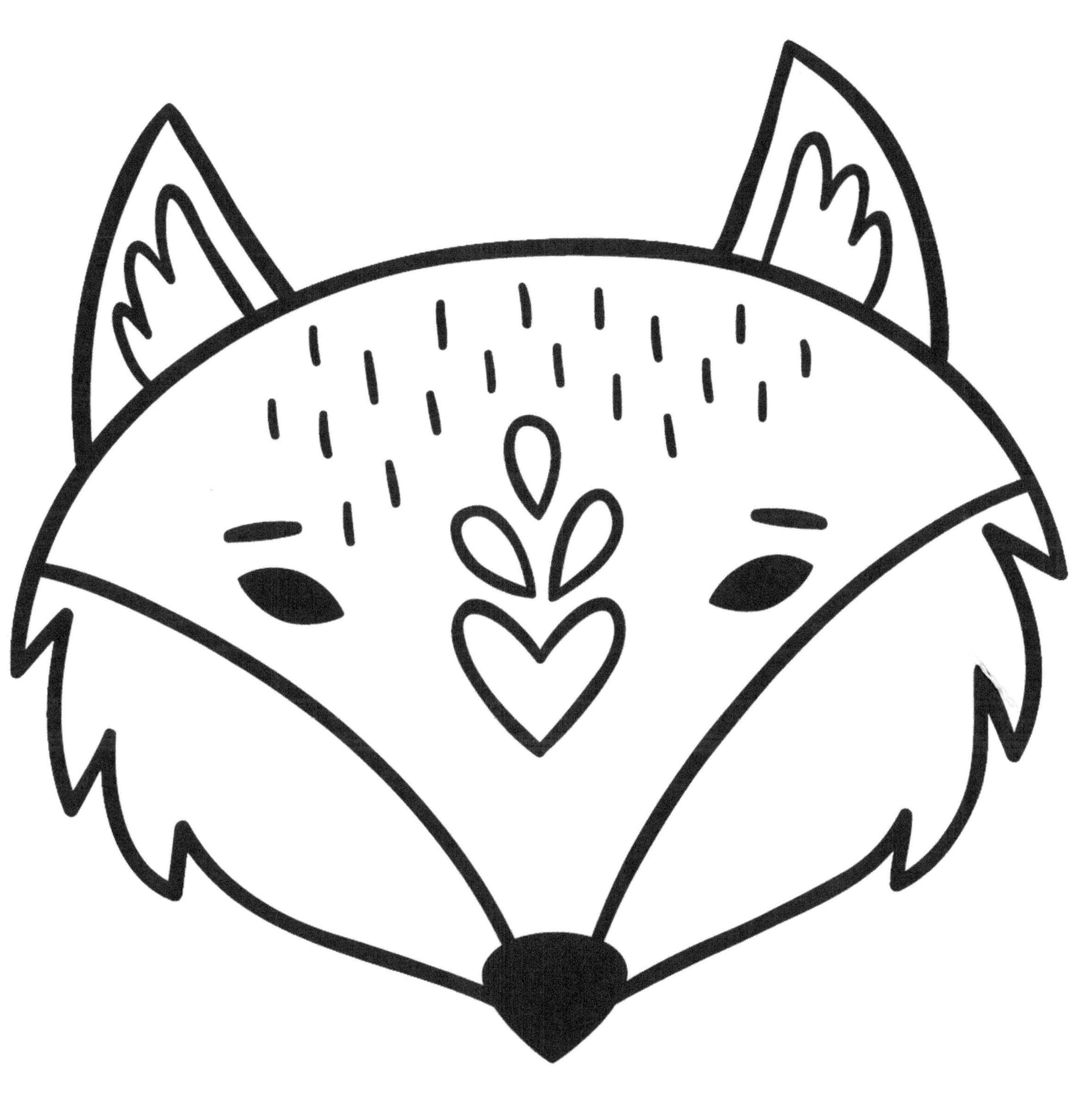

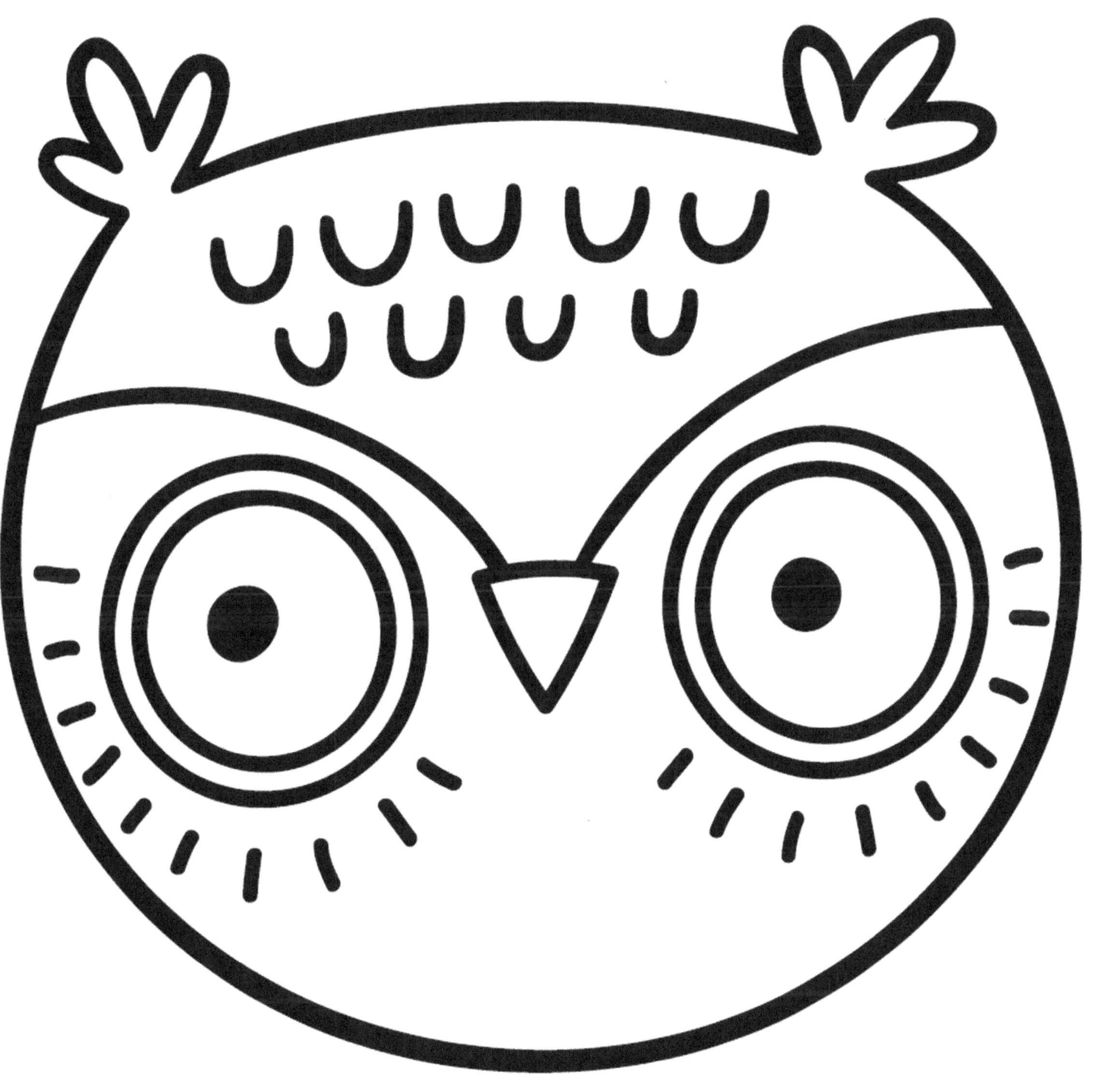

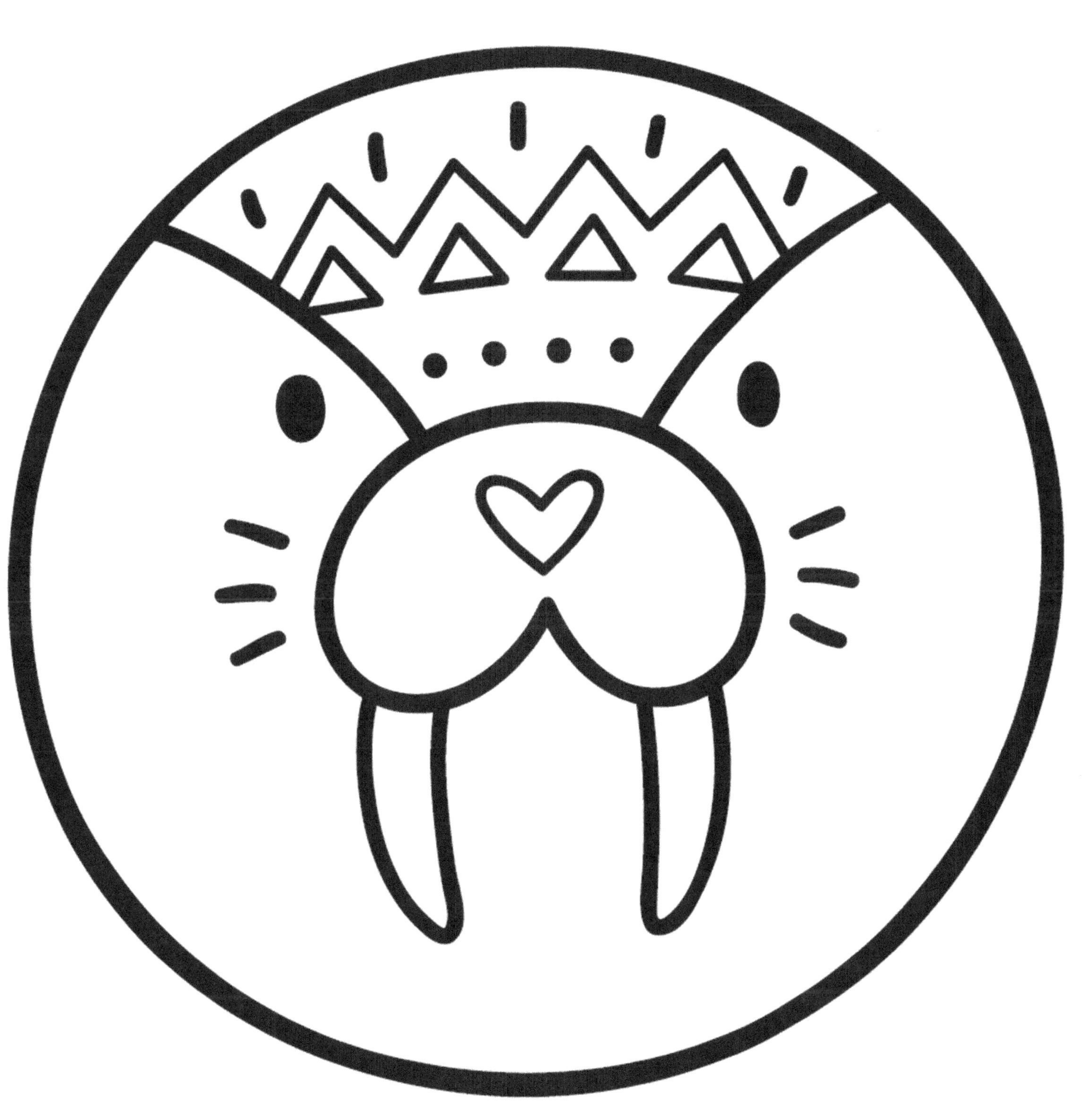

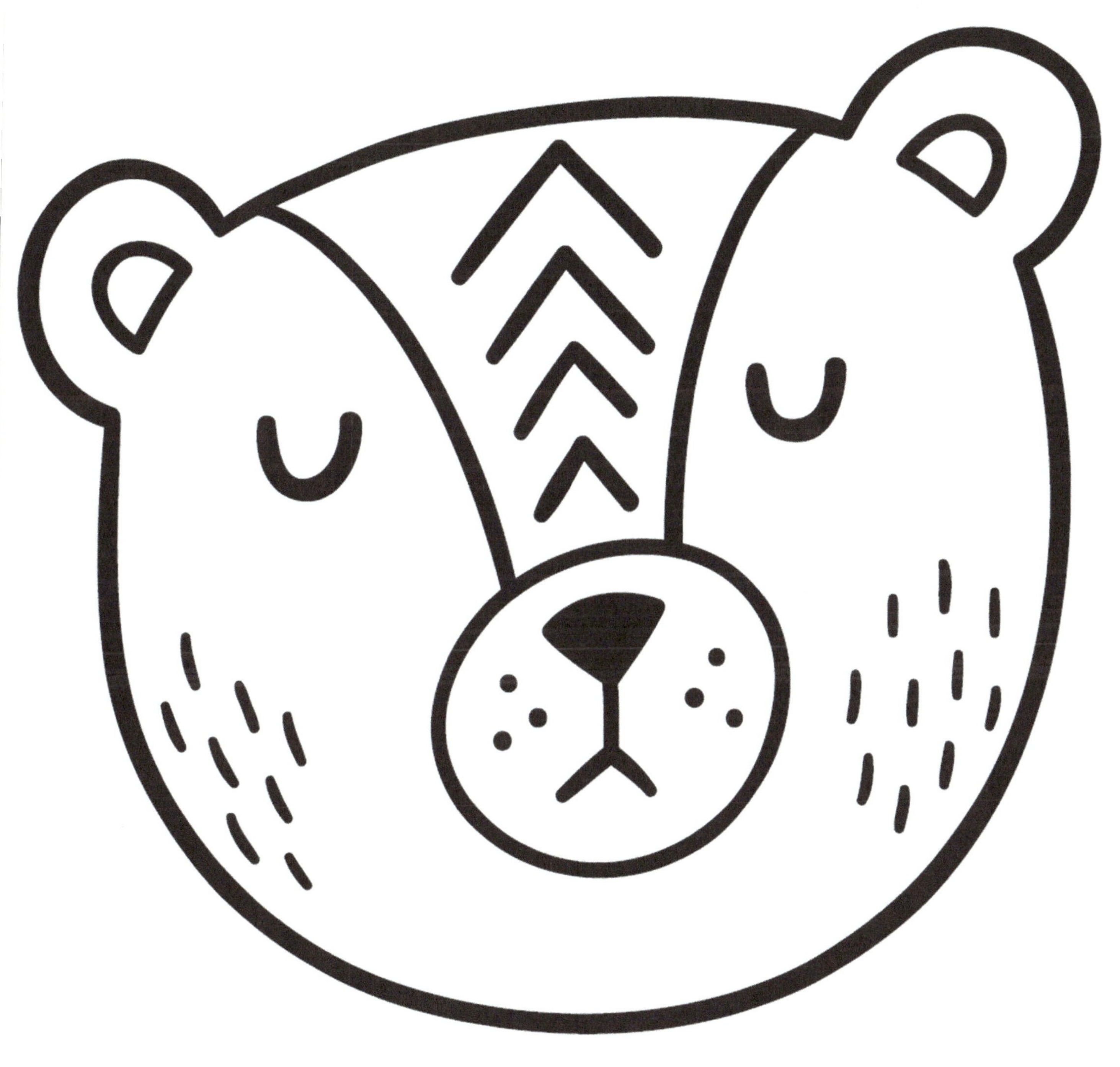

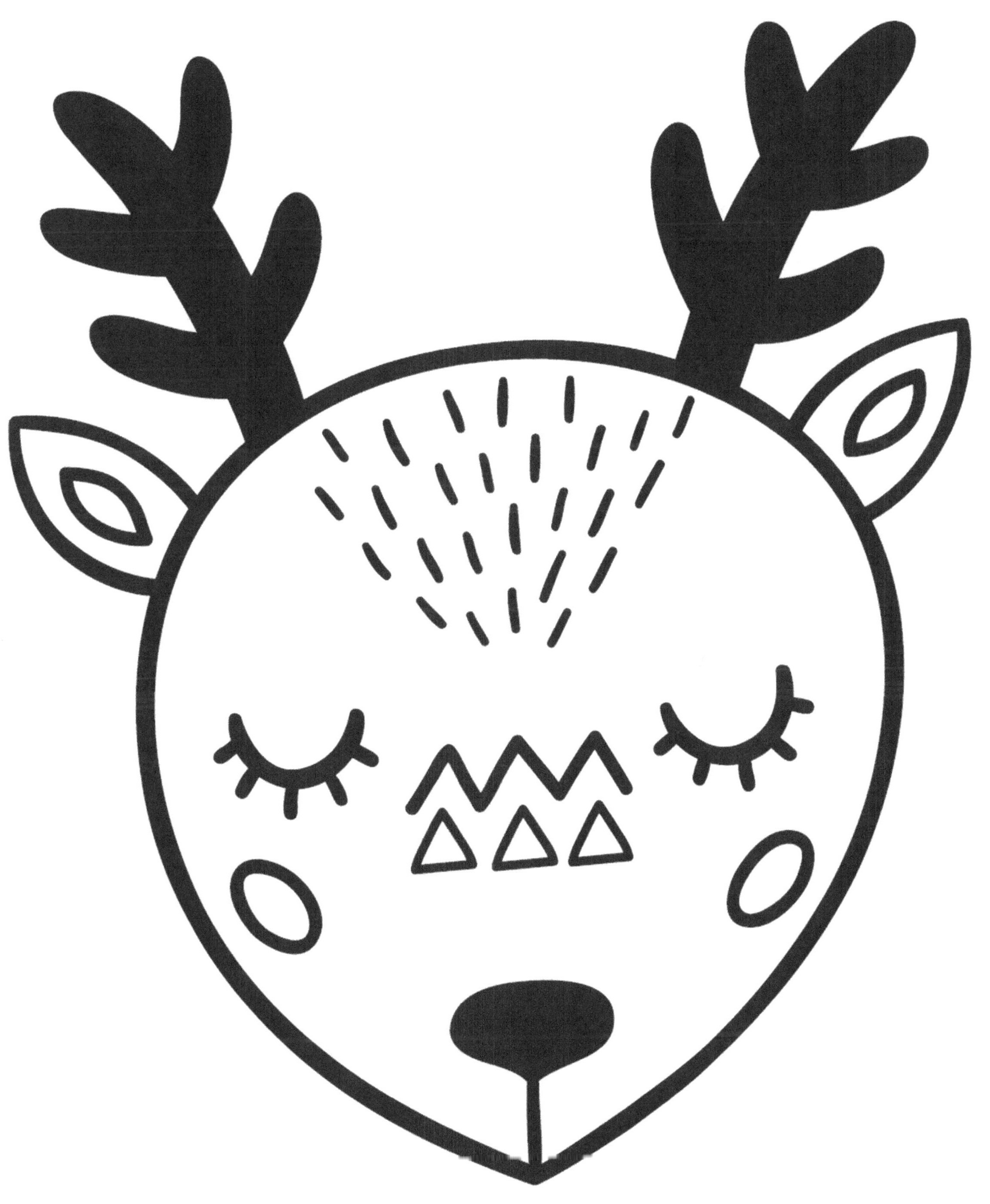

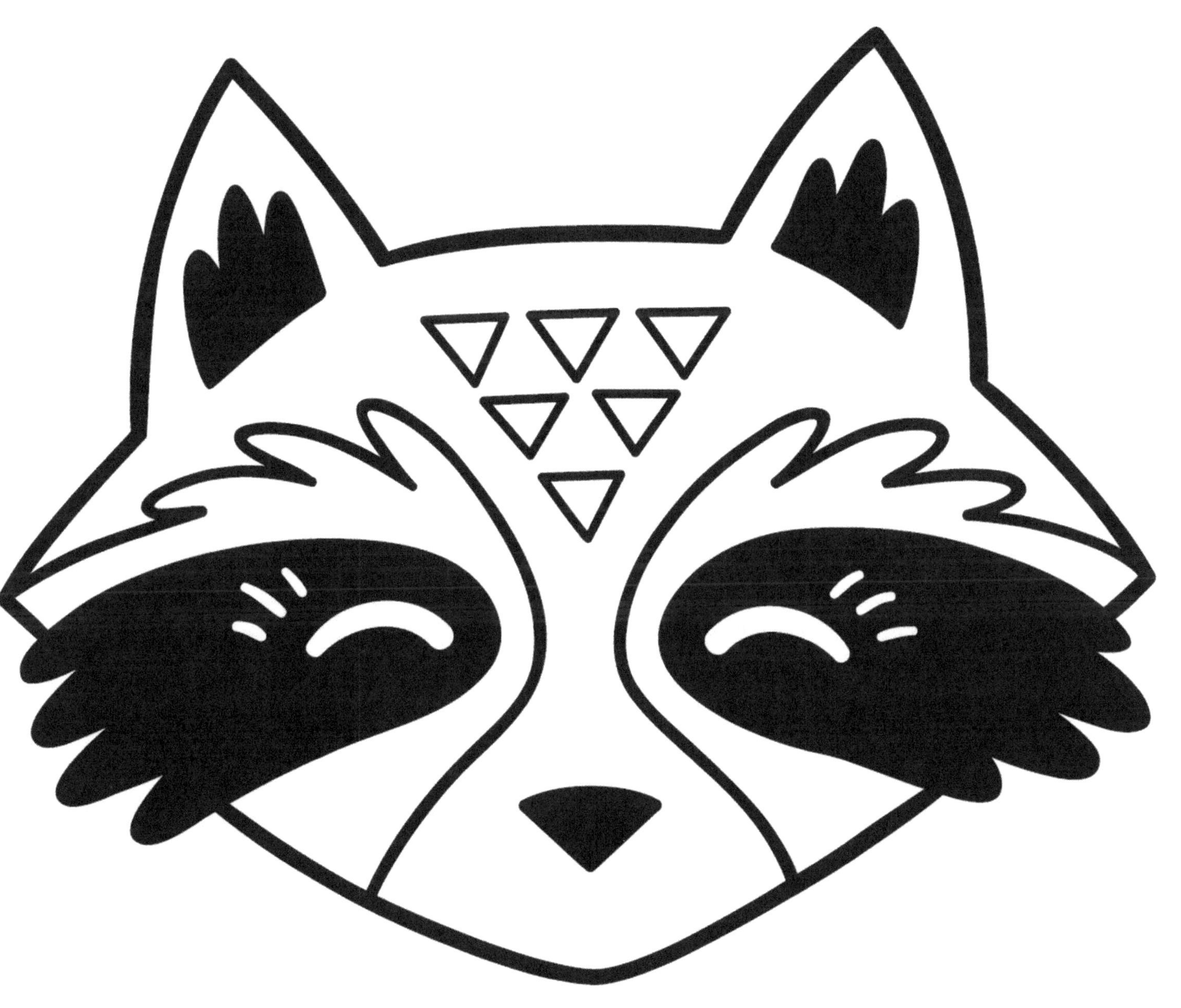

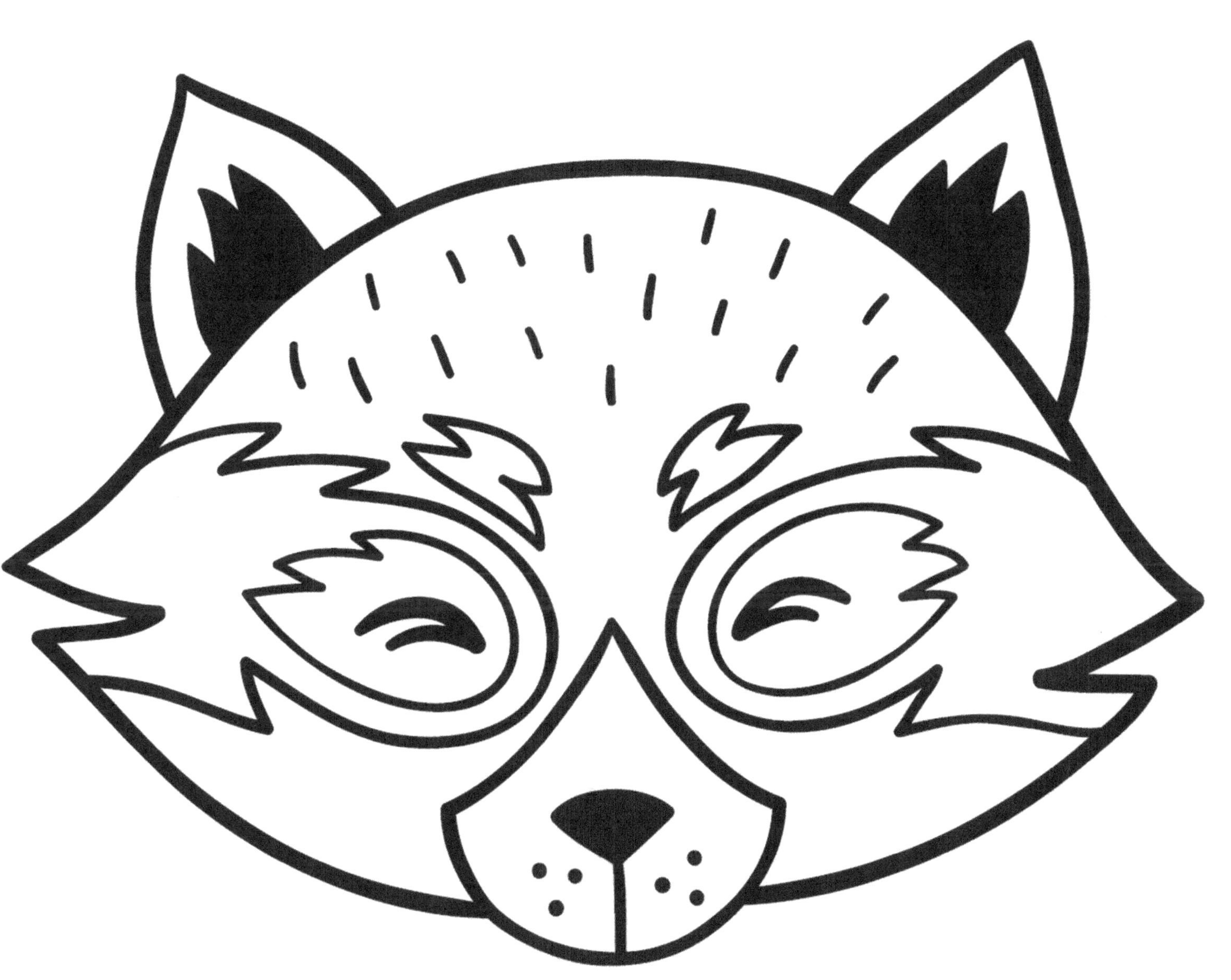

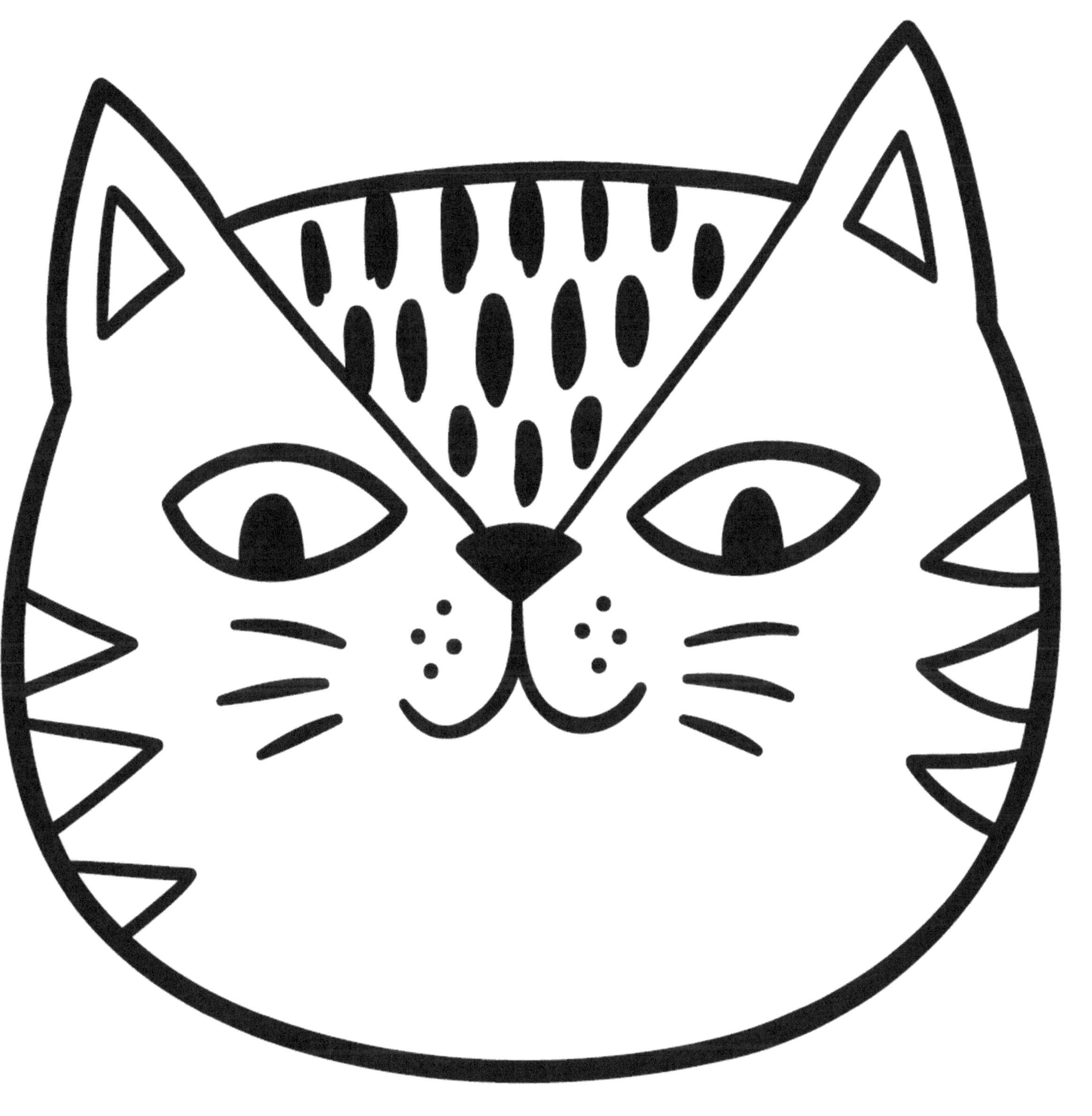

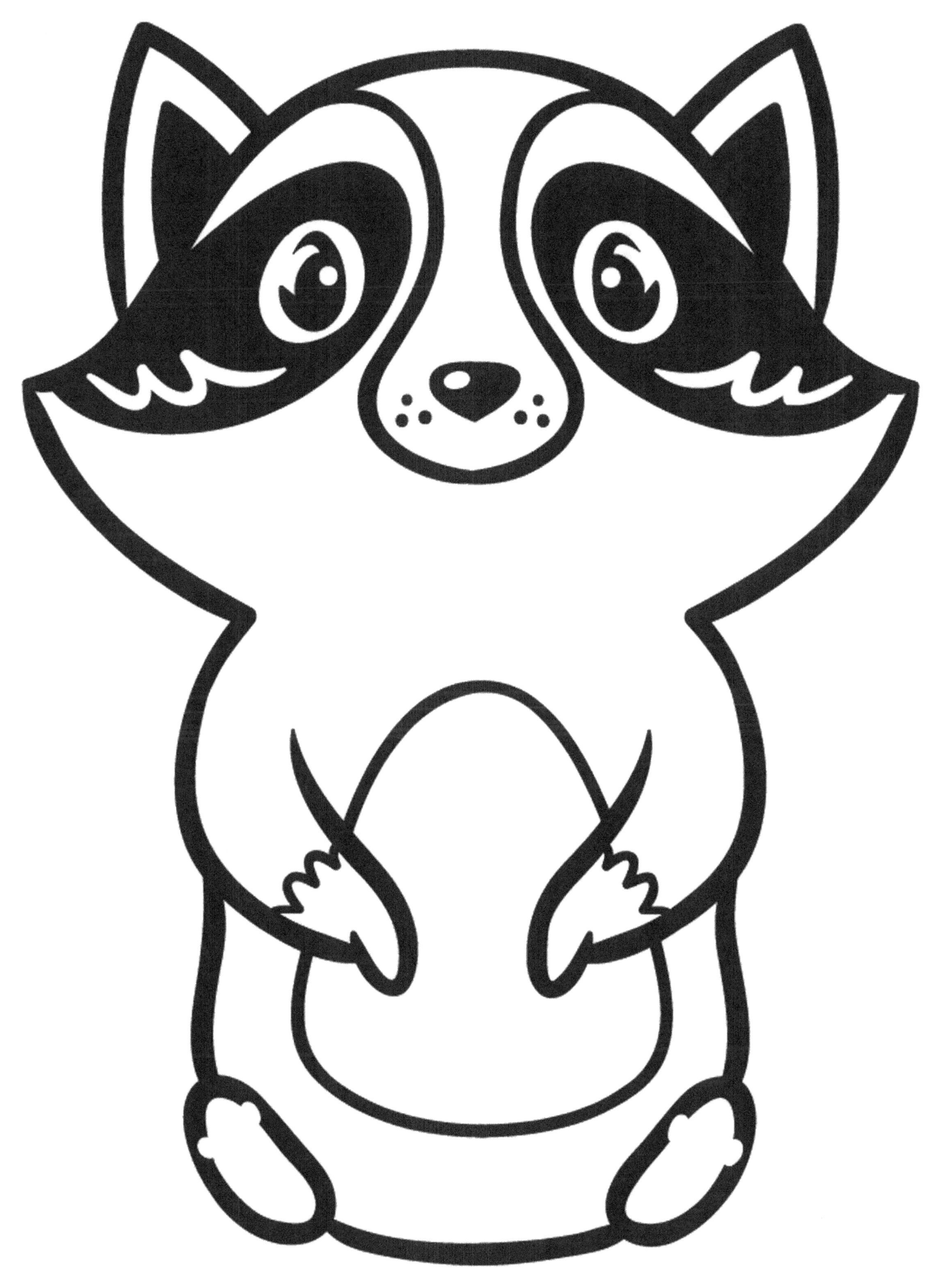

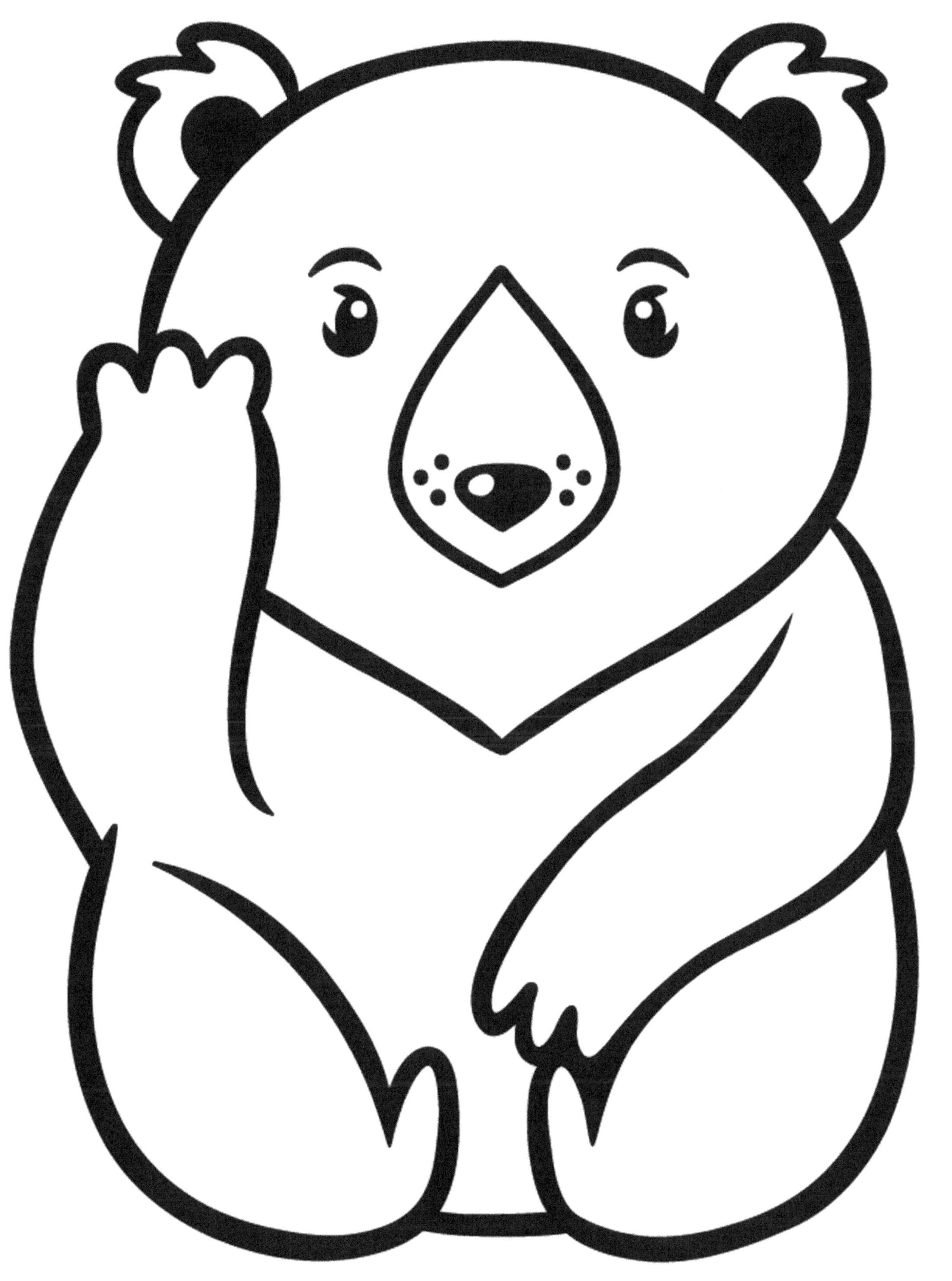

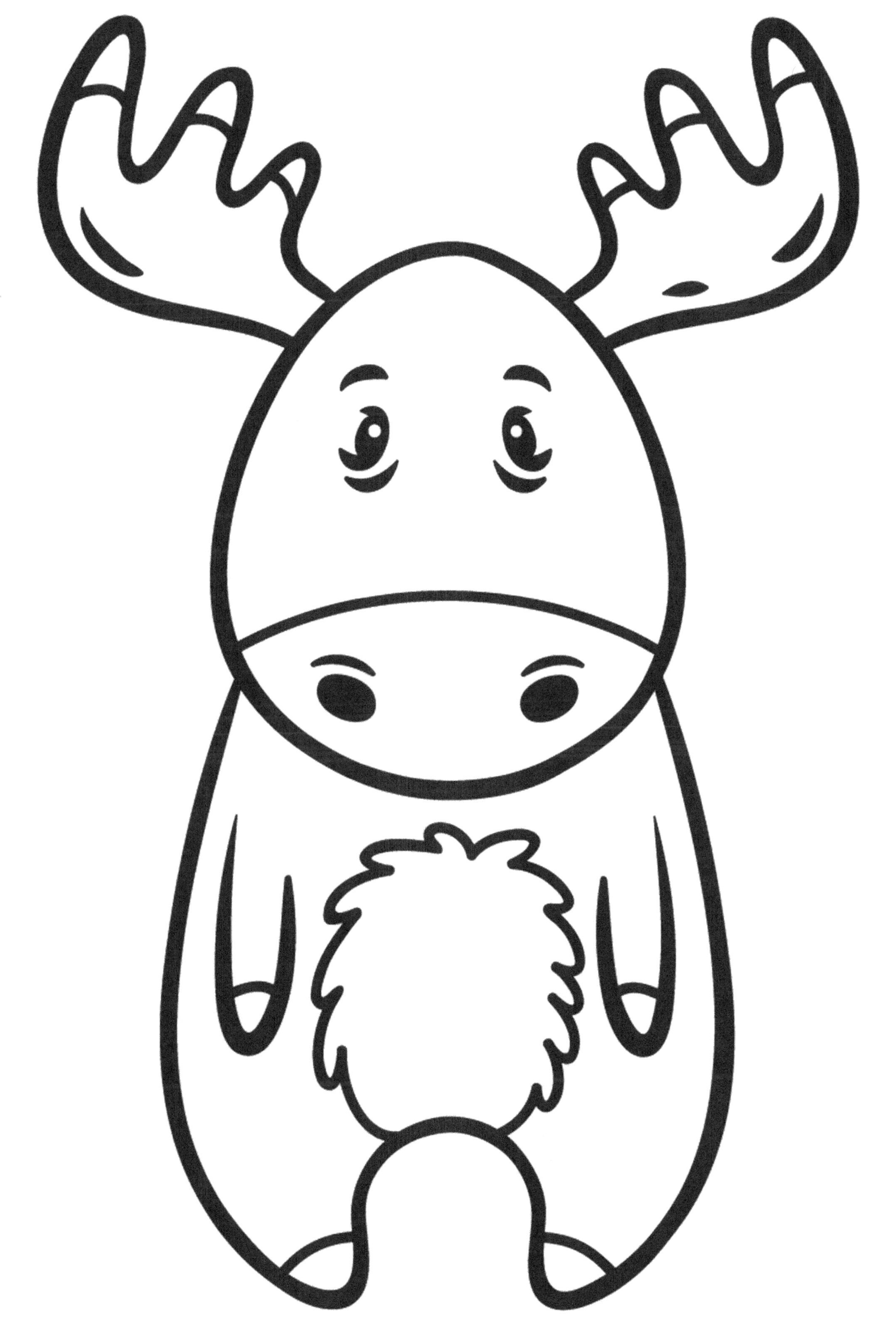

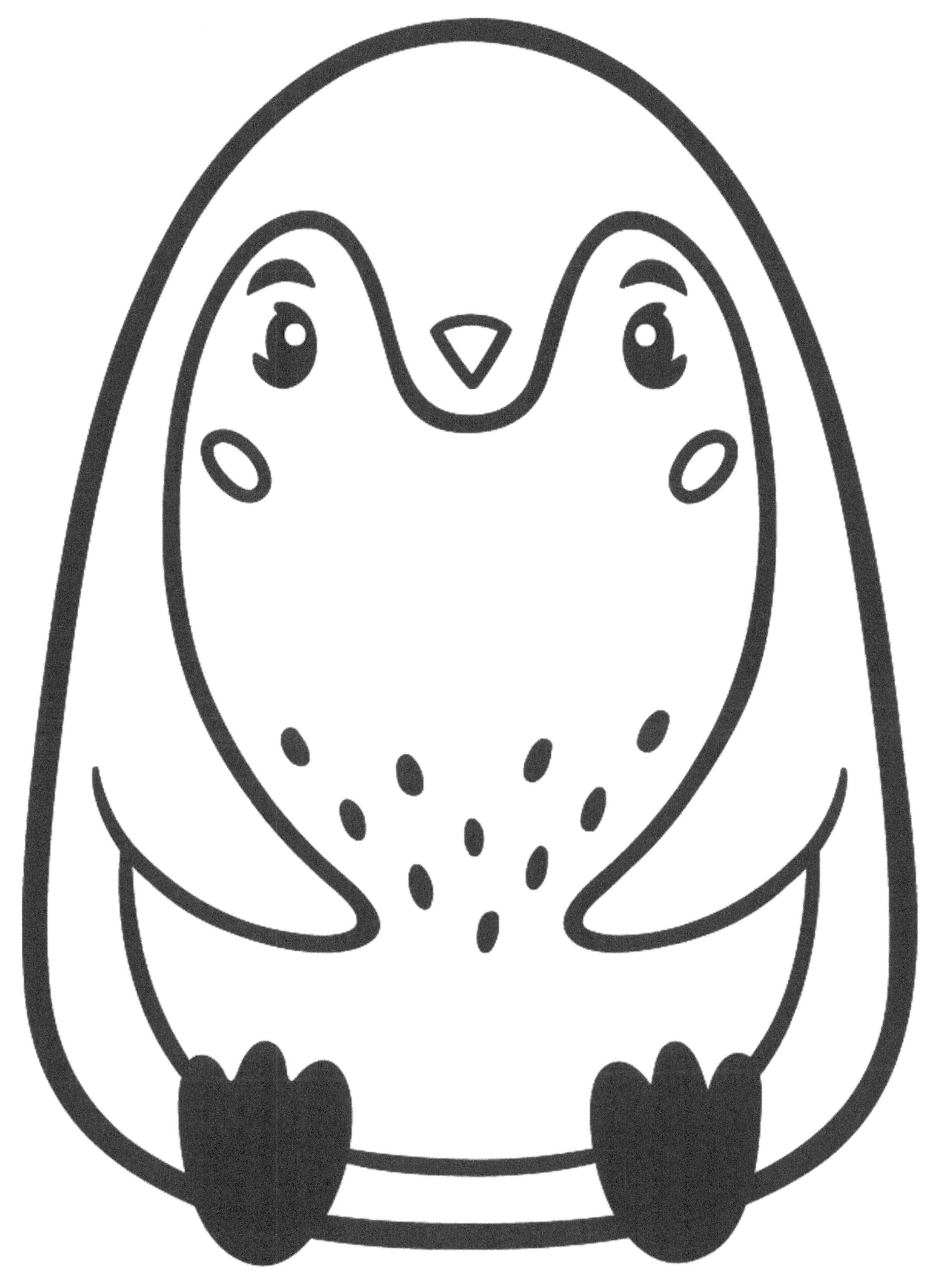

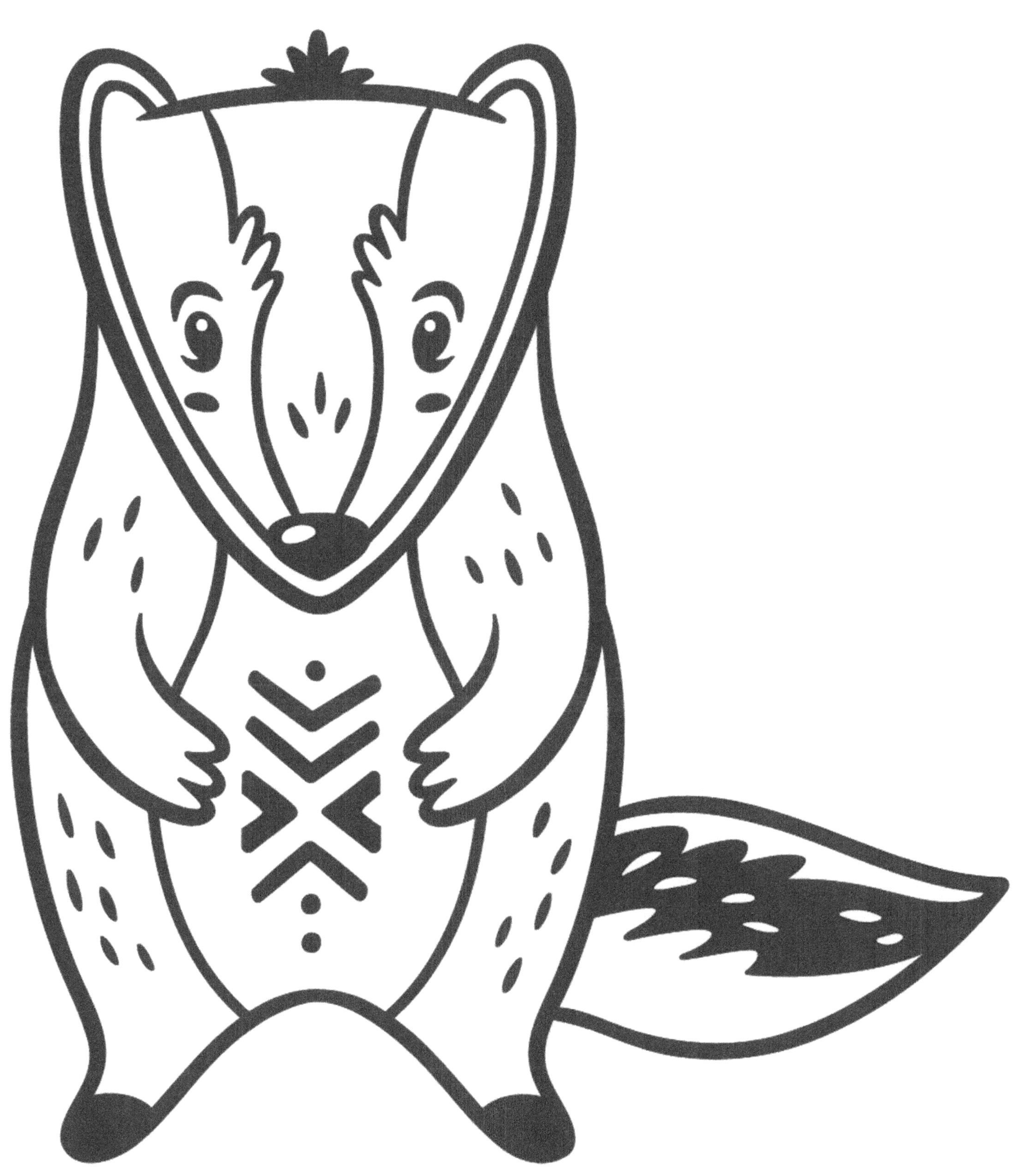

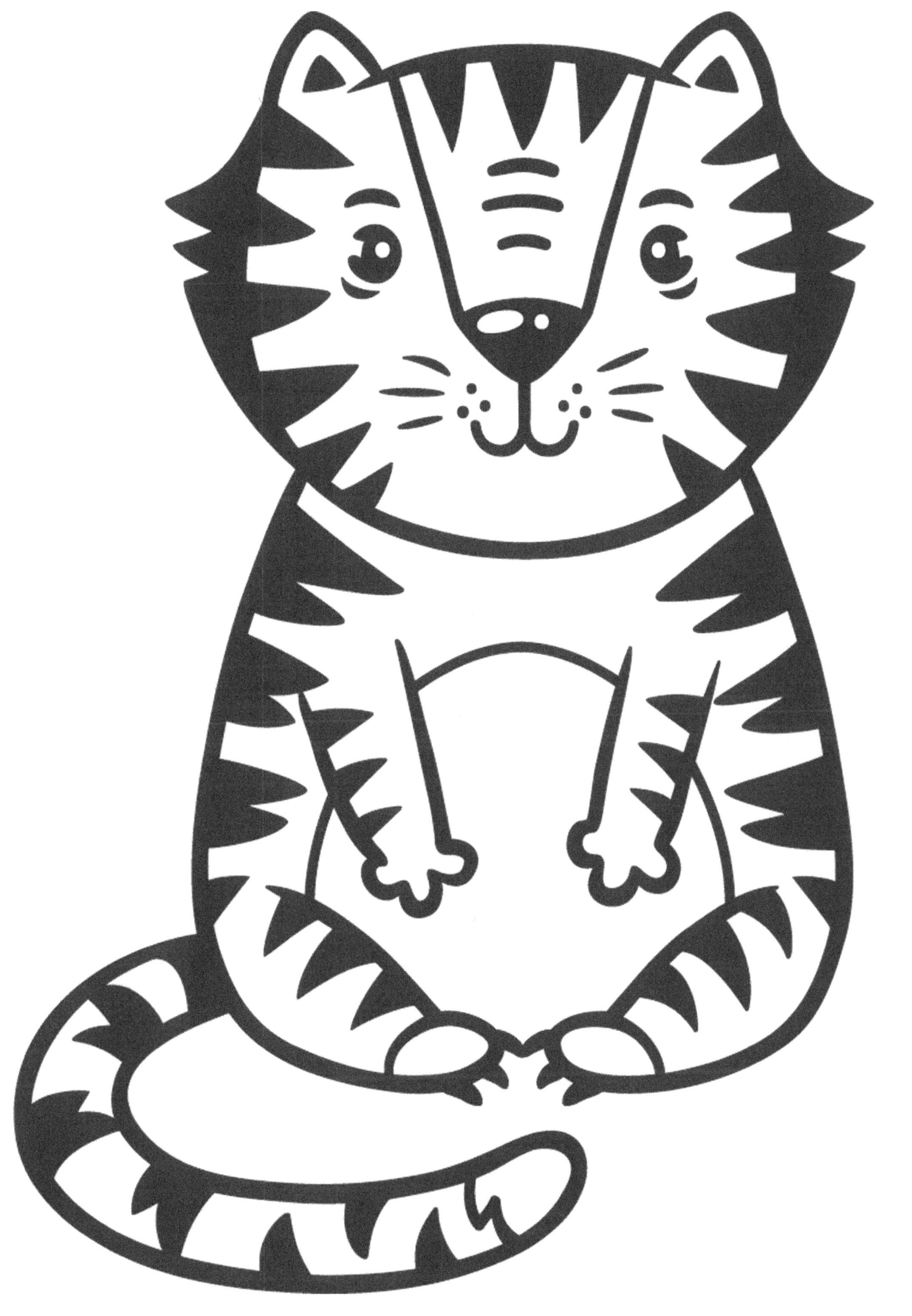

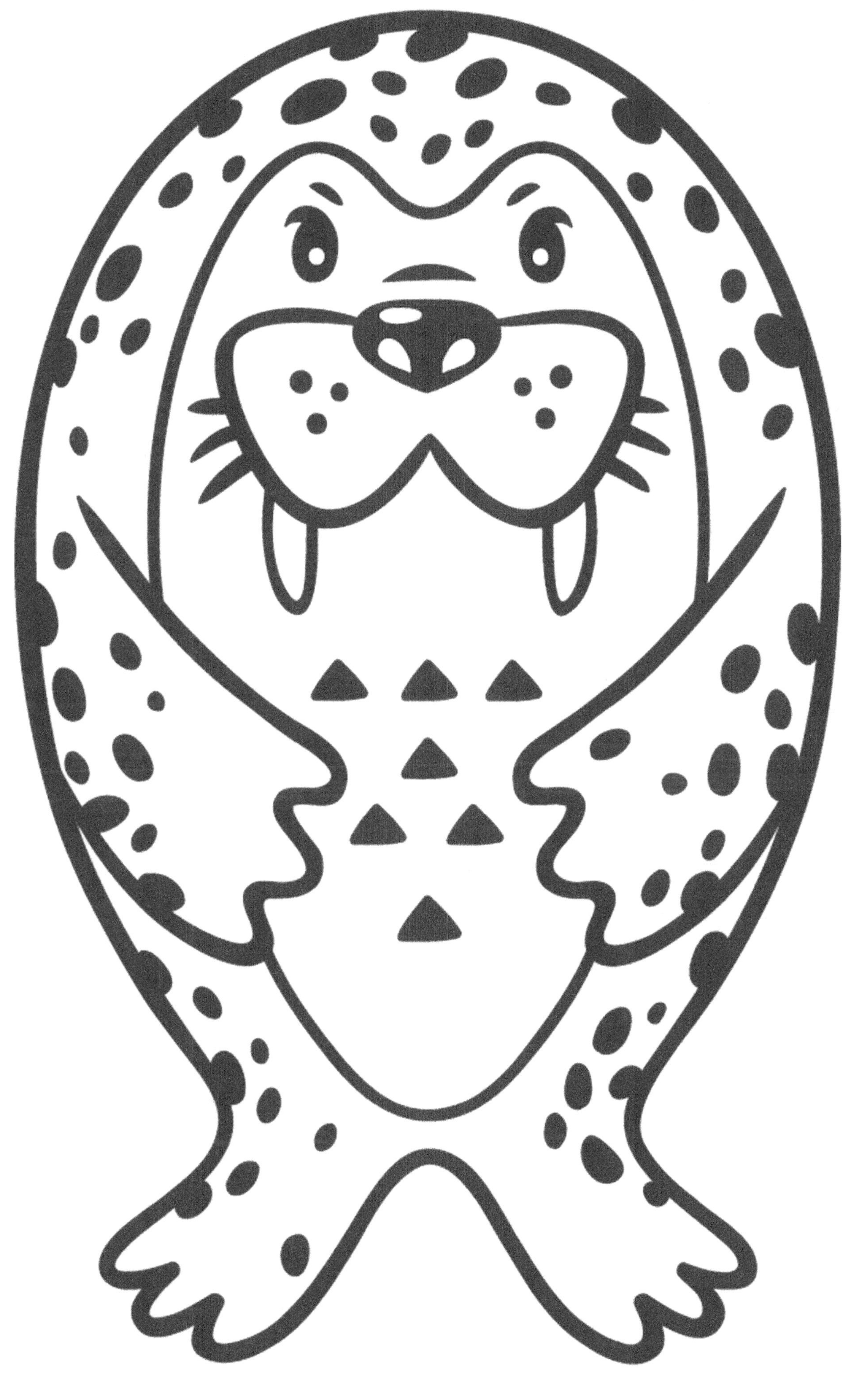

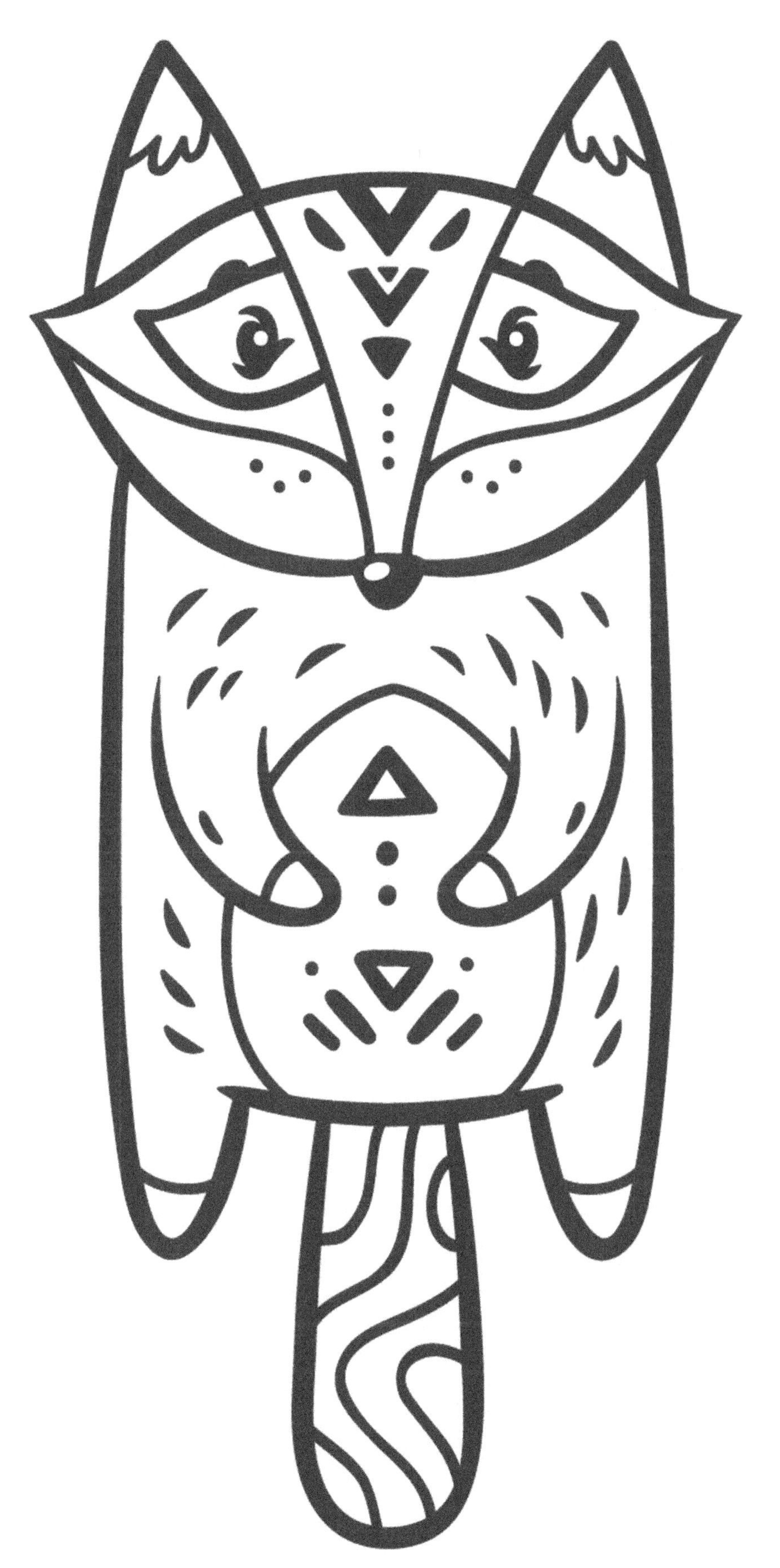

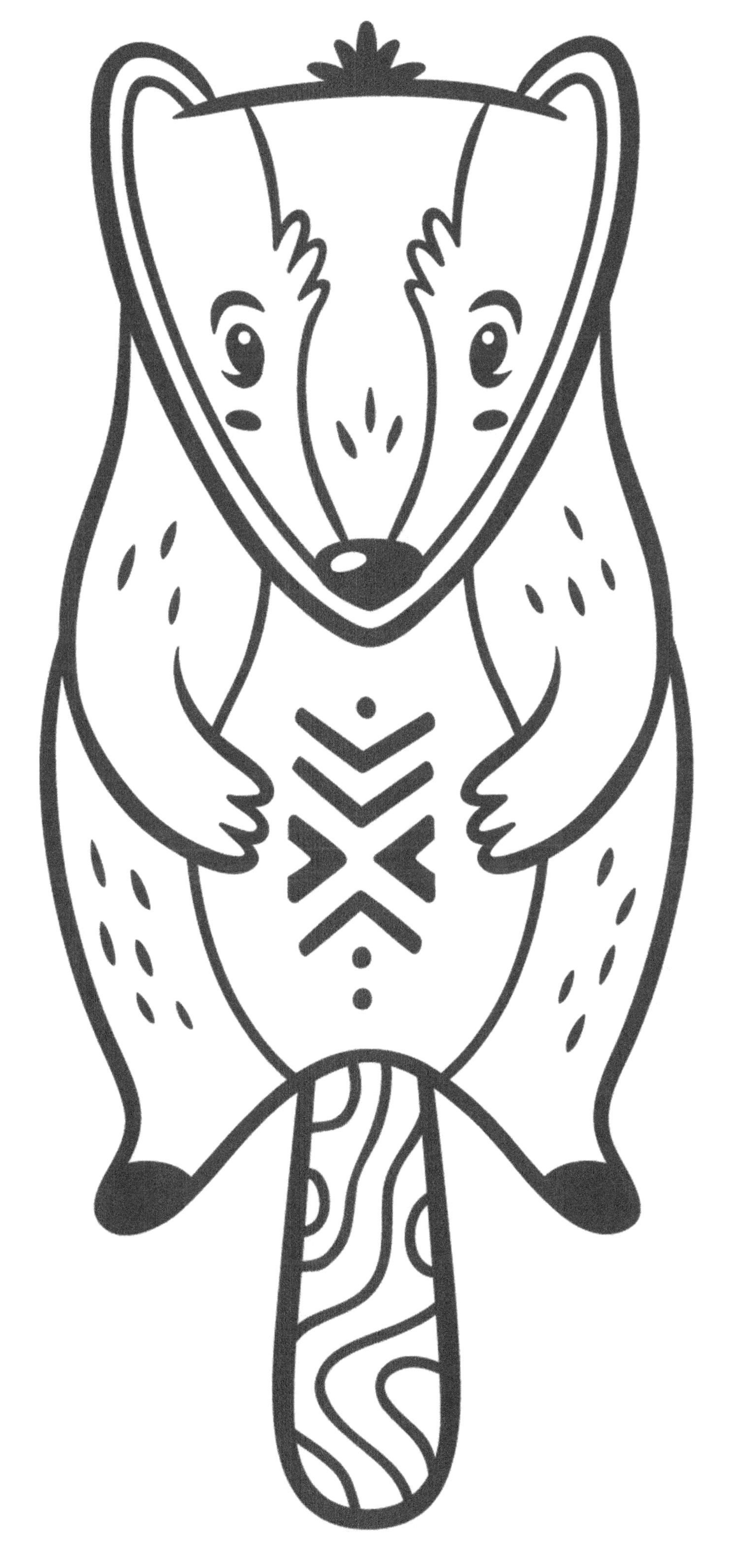

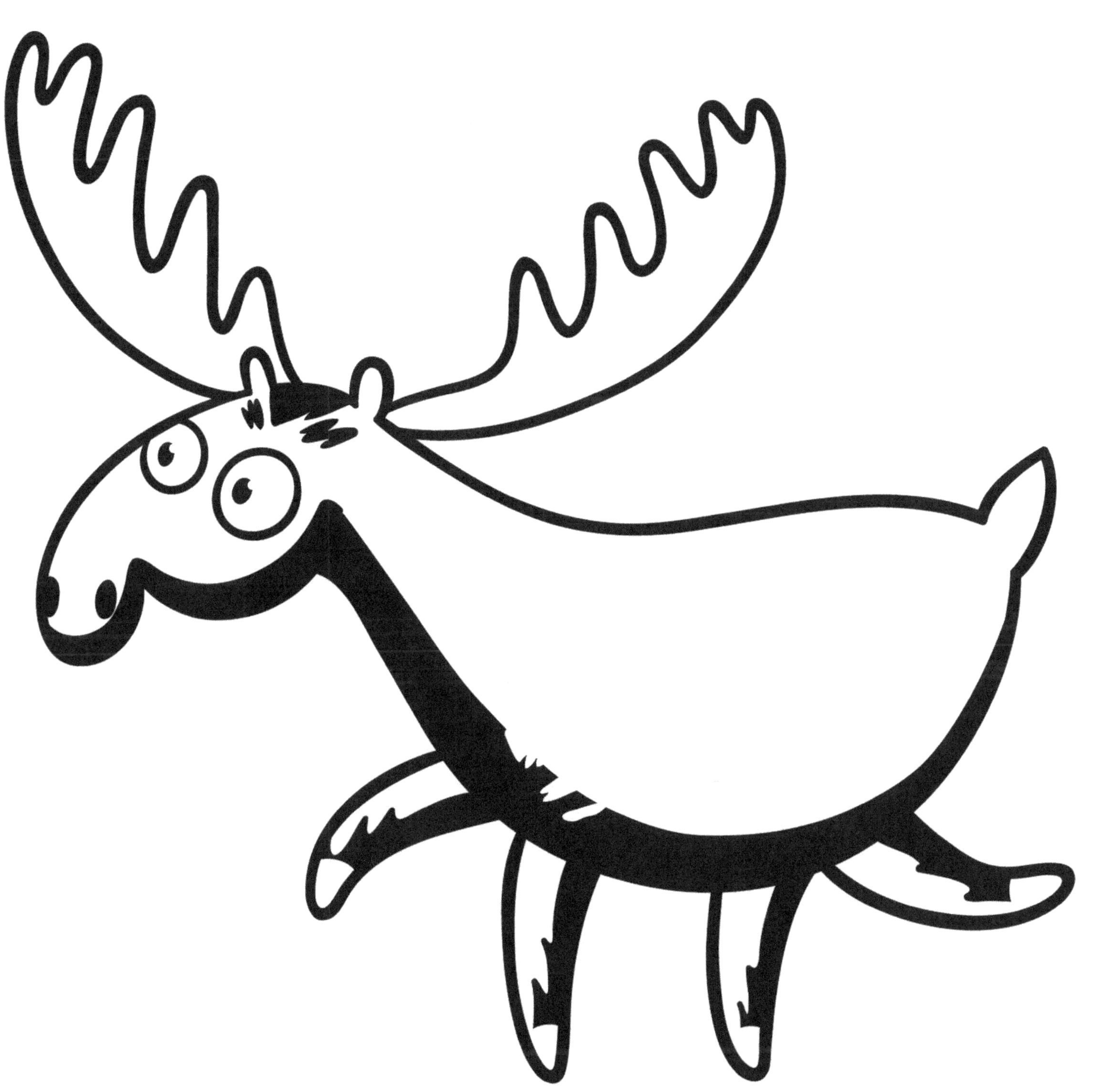

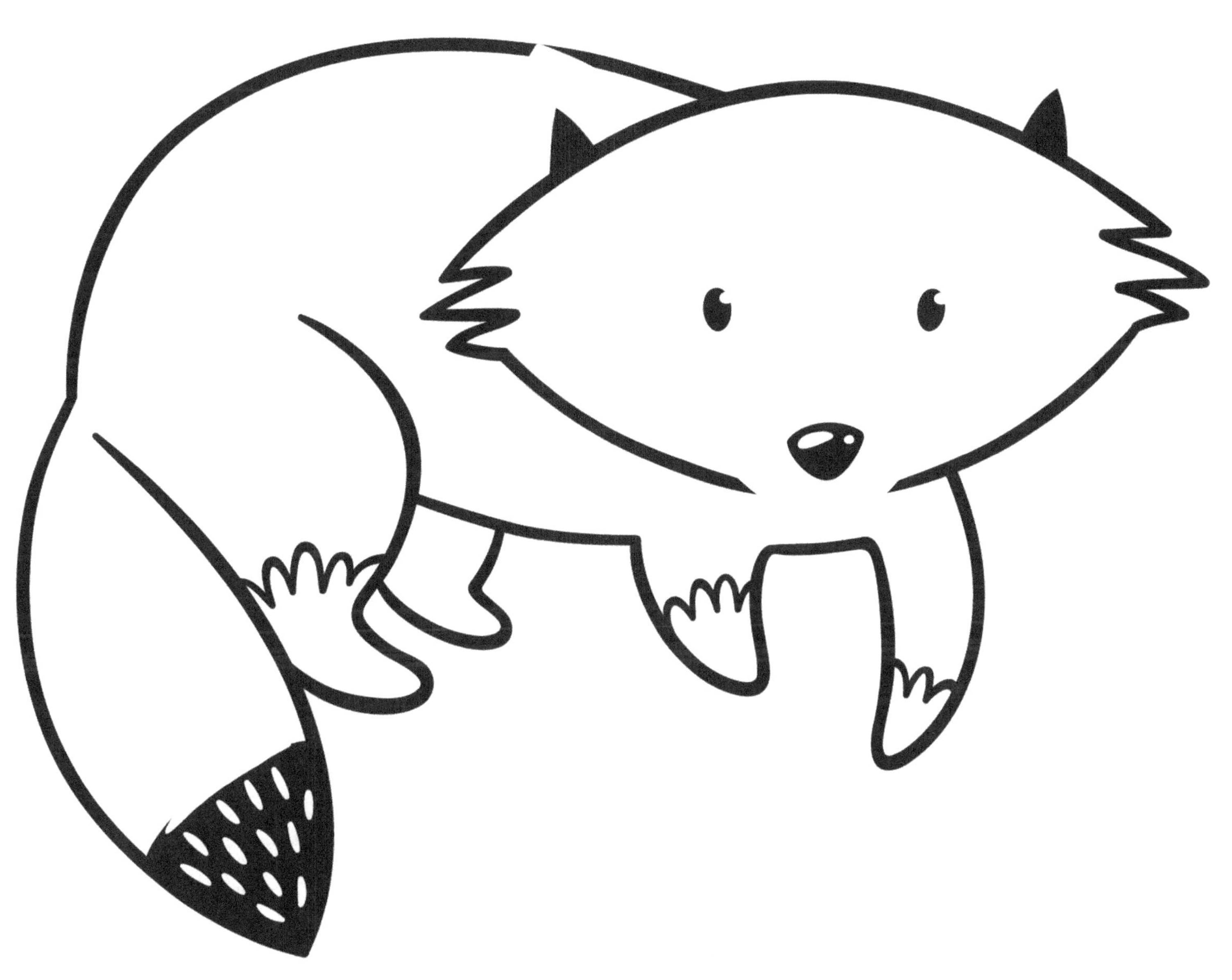

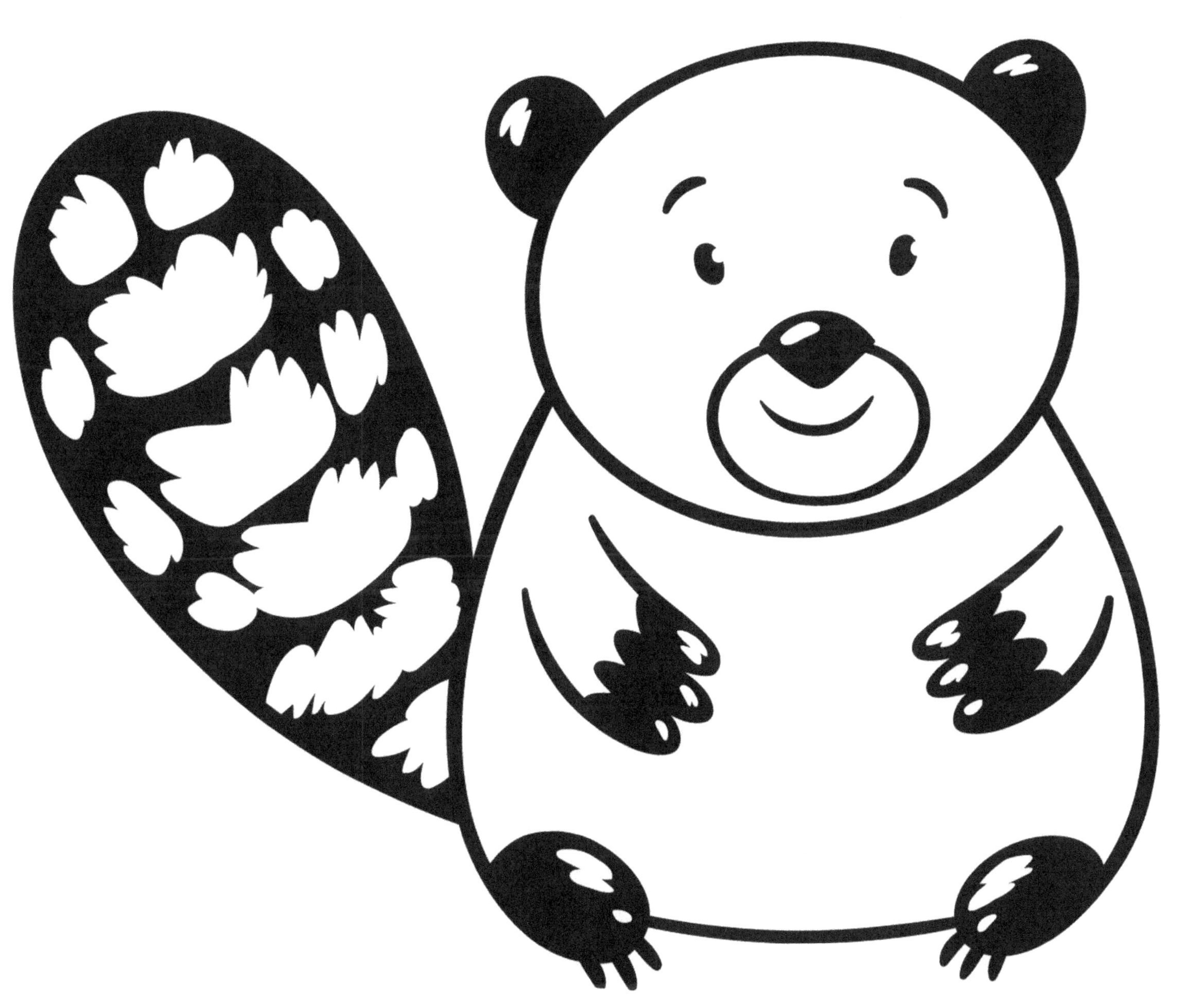

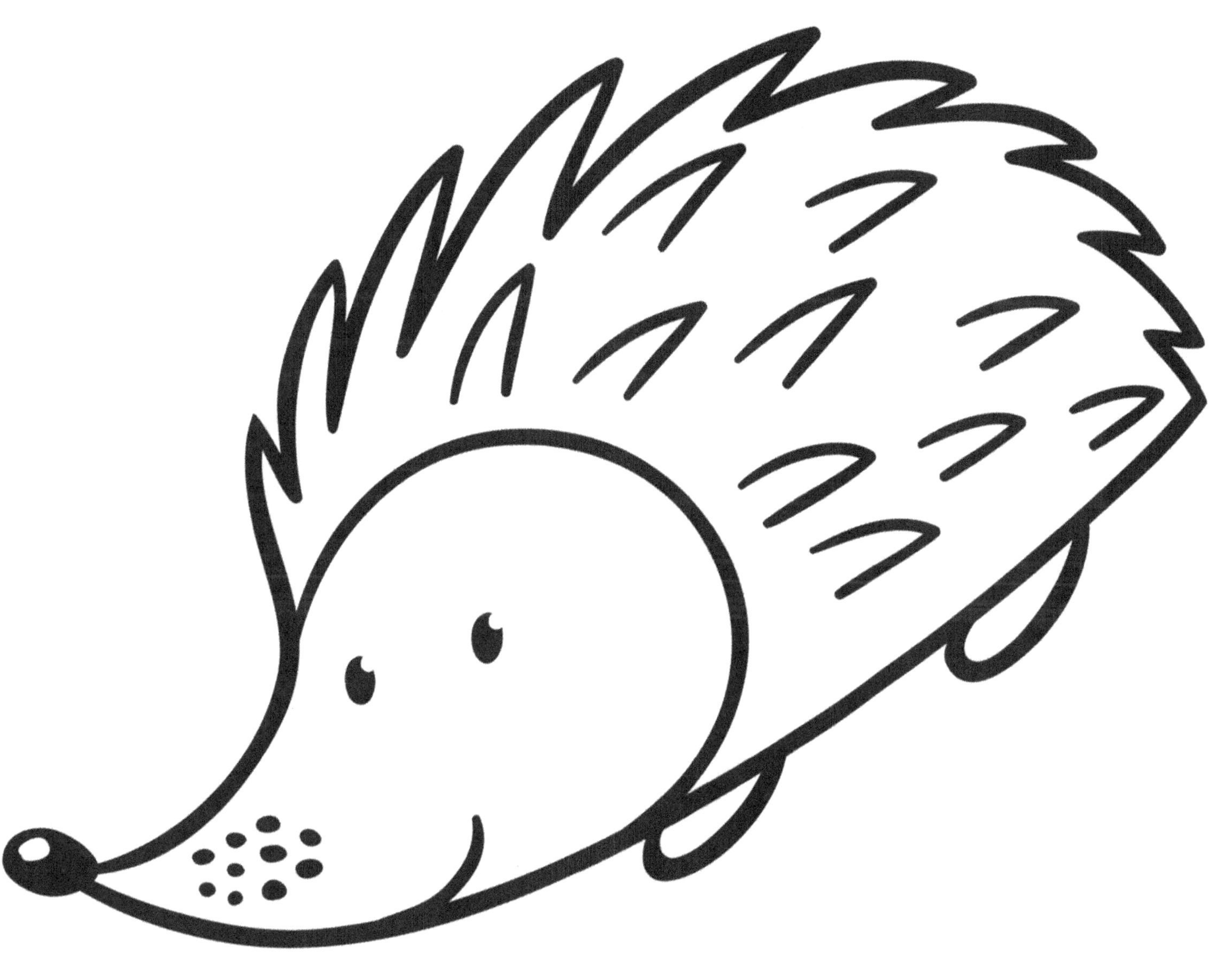

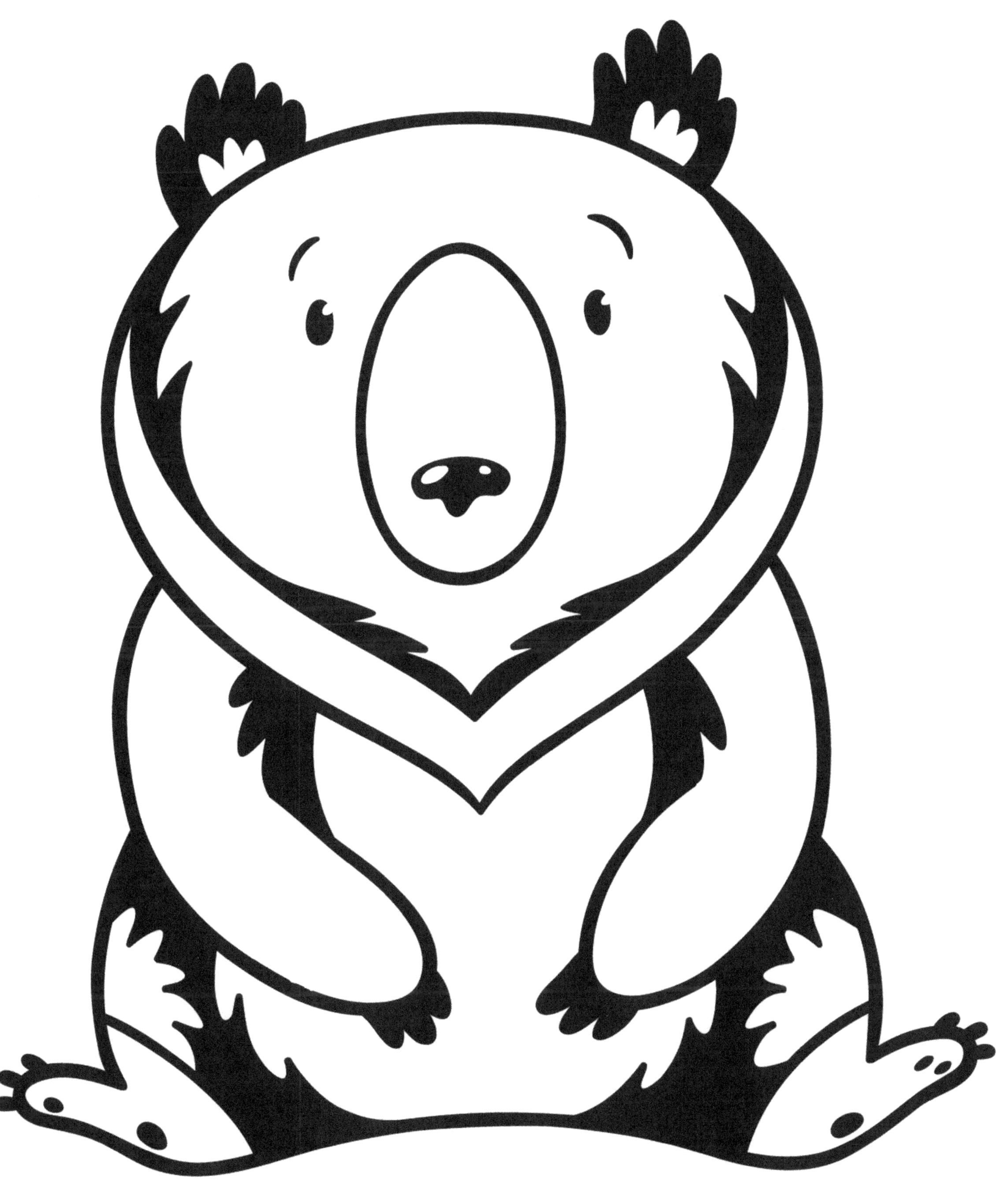

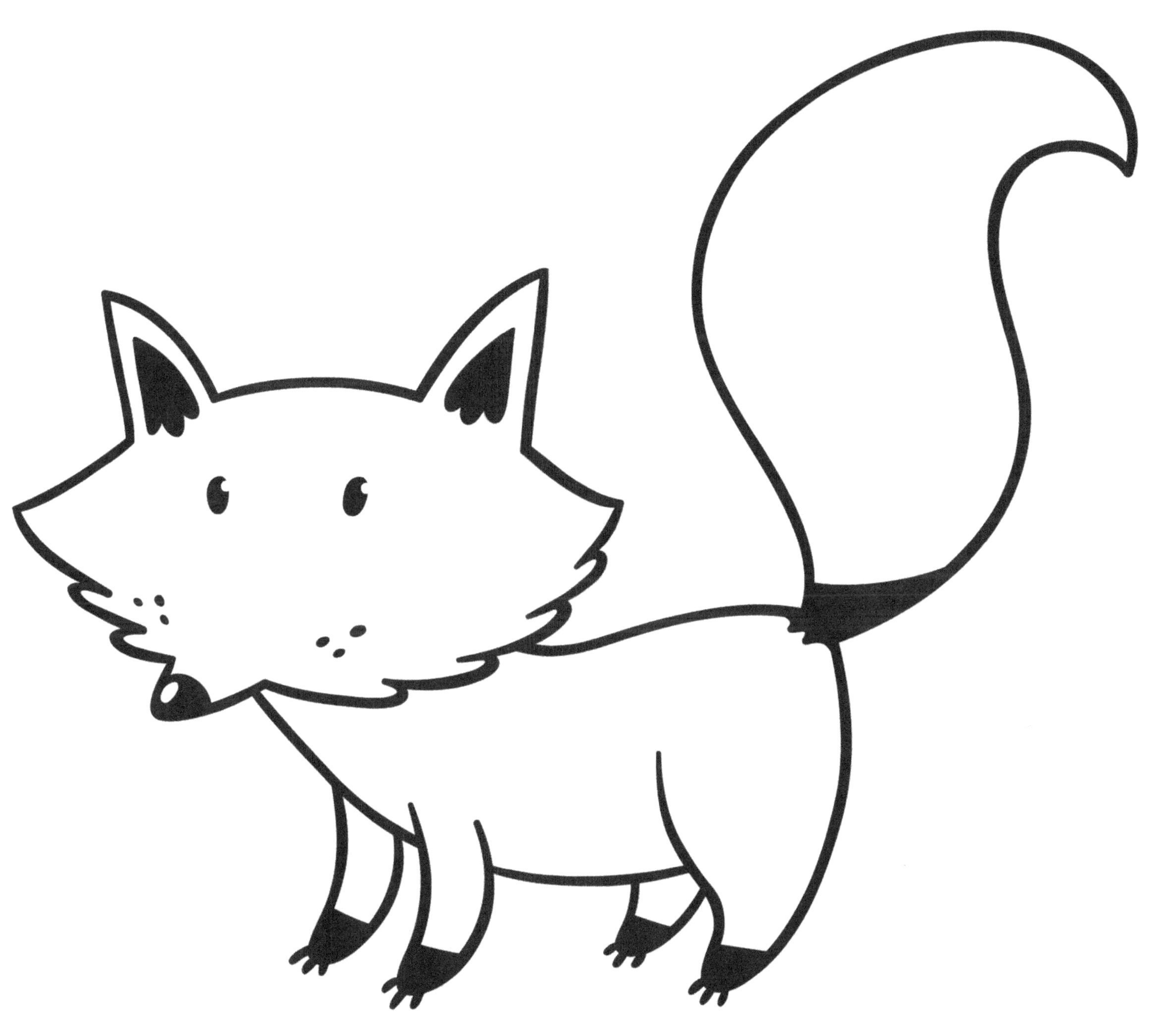

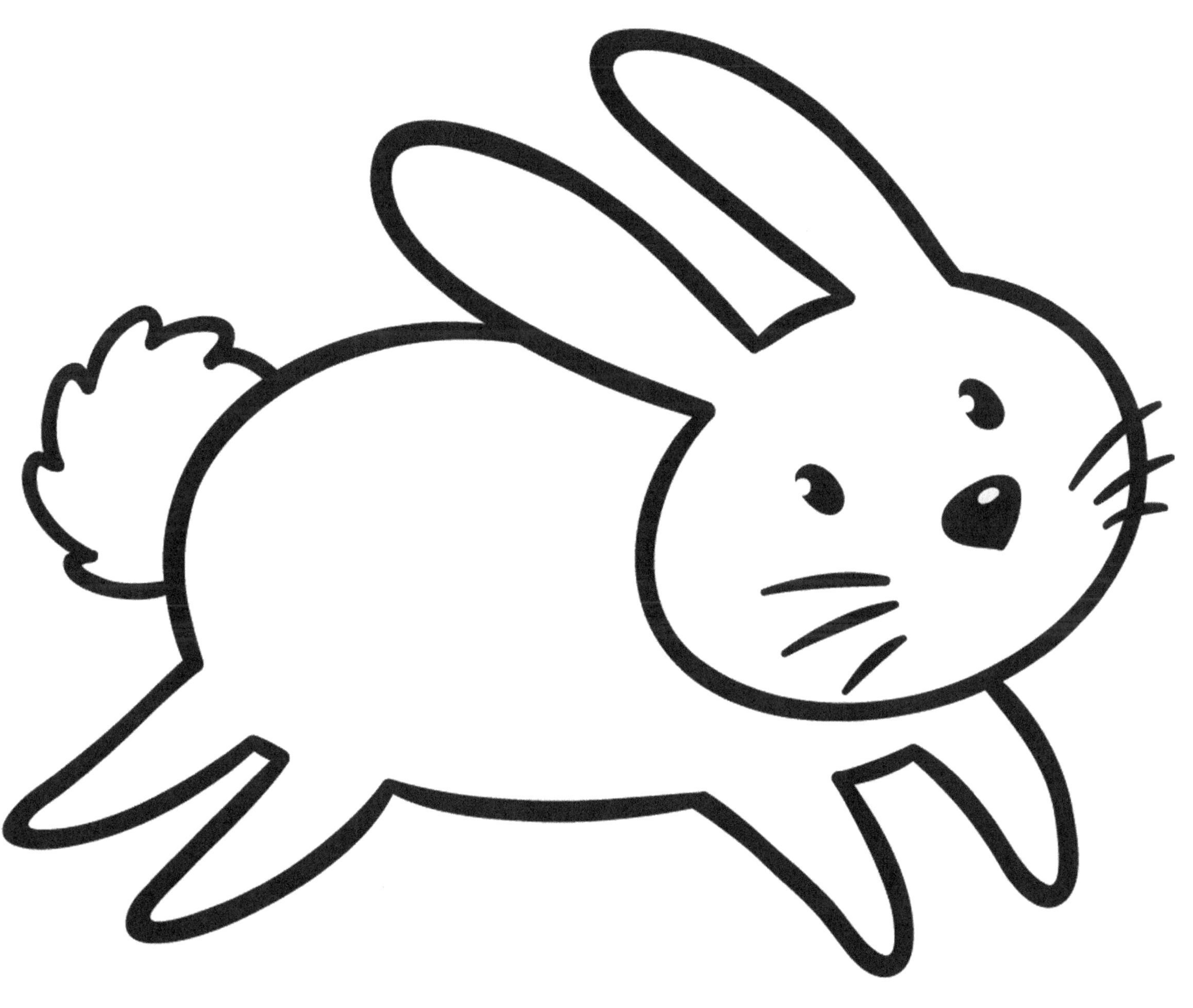

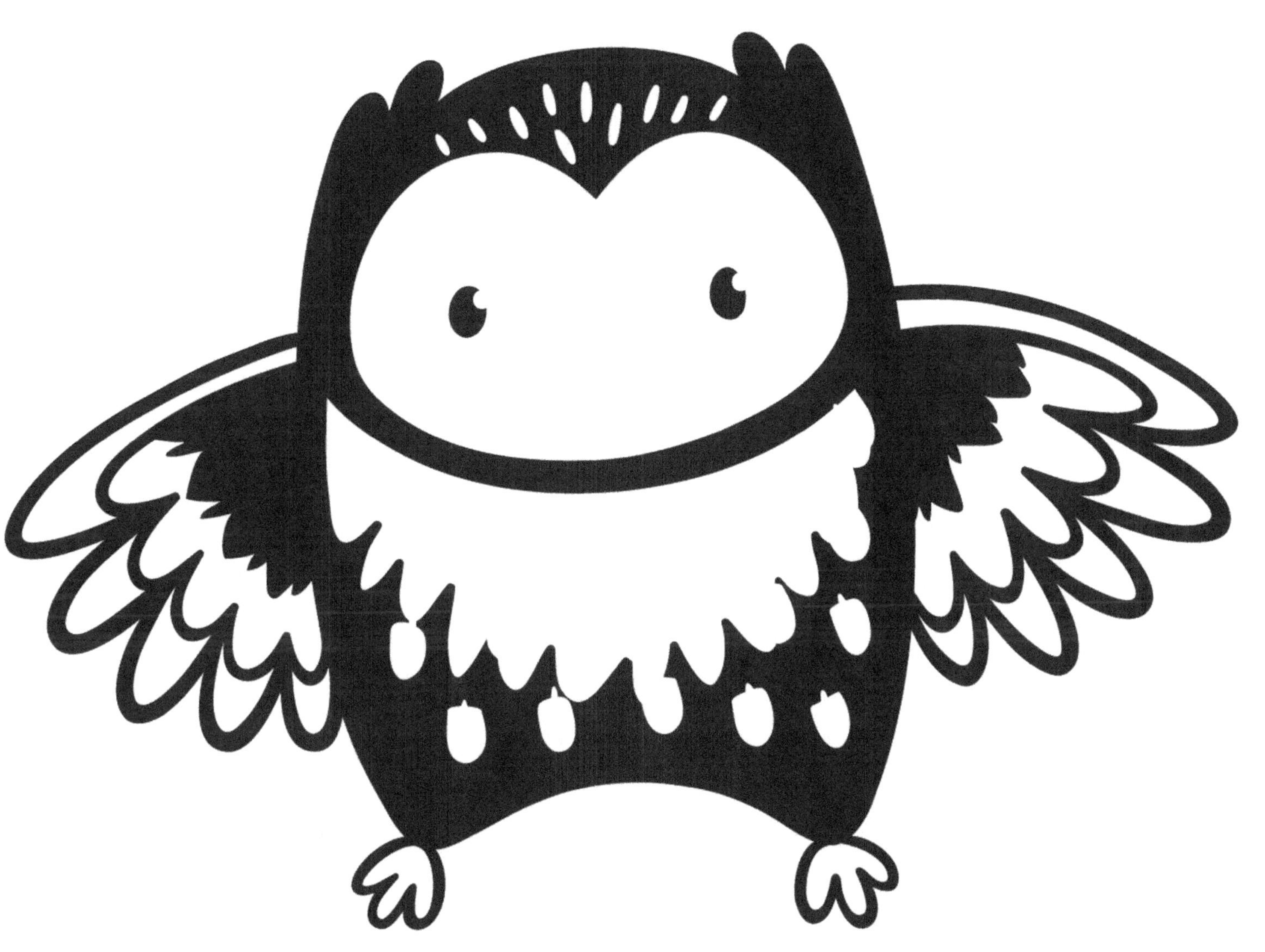

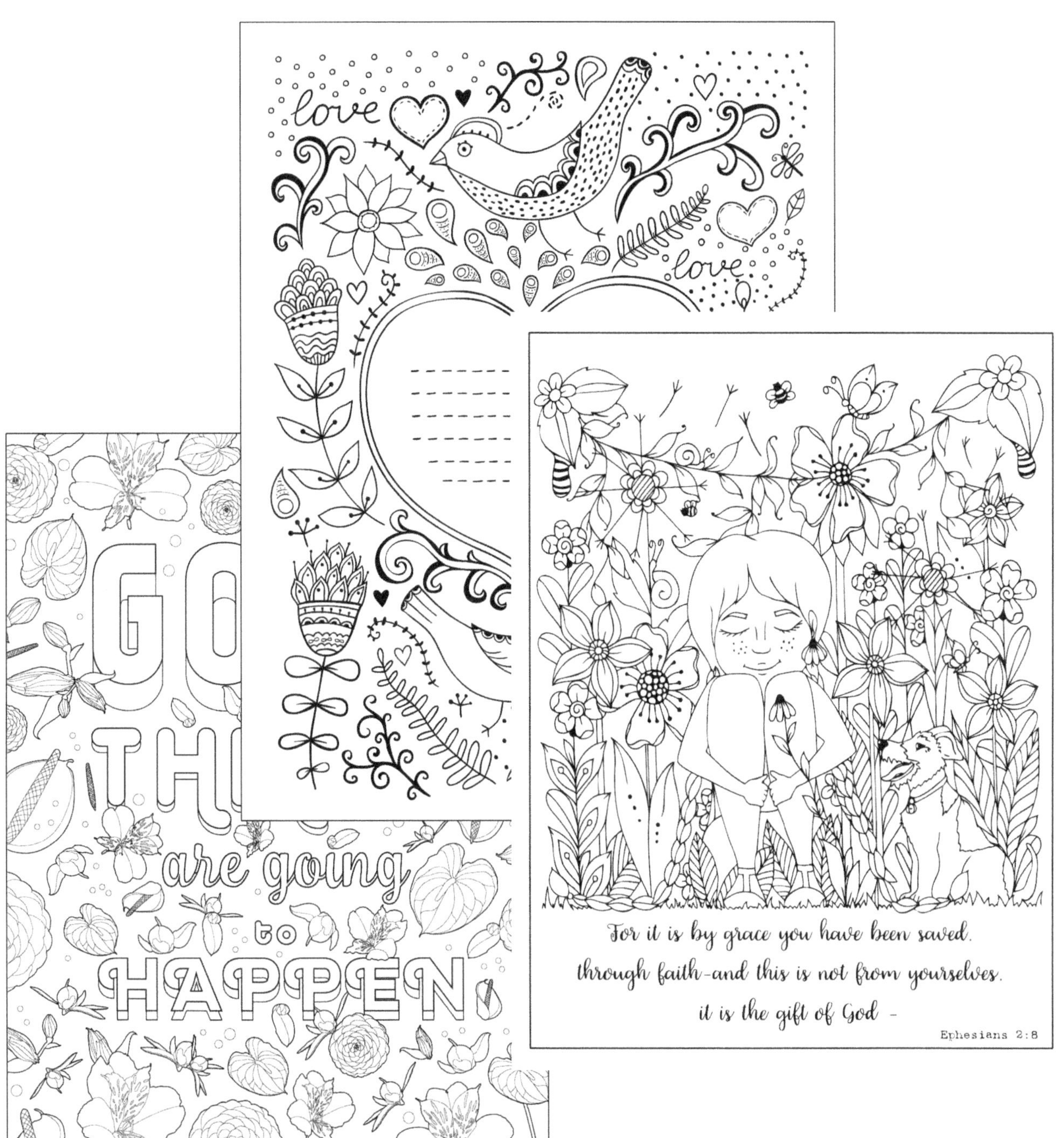

free download coloring pages

At : bit.ly/get_sample_free